Port of Leaving

poems by

Roberto Christiano

Finishing Line Press
Georgetown, Kentucky

Port of Leaving

Copyright © 2022 by Roberto Christiano
ISBN 978-1-64662-877-3 First Edition
All rights reserved under International and Pan-American Copyright Conventions.
No part of this book may be reproduced in any manner whatsoever without written
permission from the publisher, except in the case of brief quotations embodied in
critical articles and reviews.

ACKNOWLEDGMENTS

Finishing Line Press: *Port of Leaving* was previously published as a chapbook
and consisted chiefly of the Father Section.

Poetry Quarterly: "Hitler's Trains"

Prairie Schooner: "Why I Sang At Dinner"

The Ekphrastic Review: "Saint Joseph and The Boy Jesus"

The Sow's Ear: "One Song"

Writer.org: "Uncle Robbie At The Thanksgiving Table"

*Gávea-Brown: A Bilingual Journal of Portuguese-American Letters and
Studies:* "Coke Memories," "Uncle Robbie is Here," "Uncle Robbie and The
Portuguese National Football Team," "About Some Fires," "Heritage," "Leap,"
"The Cartography of Portugal," "The Wars of Rosemary and Marjoram,"
"Blues of Longing," "Memoir," "On Hearing The Fado O Gente Da Minha
Terra," "Destino," "Alcácer-Quibir, 1578"

Publisher: Leah Huete de Maines
Editor: Christen Kincaid
Cover Art: Salir e S. Martinho do Porto by Vitor Oliveira, https://www.flickr.
com/photos/vitor107, Wikimedia Commons.
Author Photo: Mary Bley
Cover Design: Elizabeth Maines McCleavy

Order online: www.finishinglinepress.com
also available on amazon.com

Author inquiries and mail orders:
Finishing Line Press
P. O. Box 1626
Georgetown, Kentucky 40324
U. S. A.

Table of Contents

PORTUGAL AND THE WORLD

FATHER

MY FATHER IS A BRICKLAYER

Driving through Georgetown
on a congested Friday afternoon,
I find myself stopped
behind a truckload of bricks
when my father comes to me—
red brown in his Portuguese skin.
"I'm a bricklayer by trade,"
he often says,
and his hands show it—
all calloused like tree bark.
I can drive through my hometown
and show you the homes
he built with those hands and arms
and a back that bent
as he spread the mortar.
"I built my own house,"
he says, and he did—
built it with swelter
and sinewy muscle,
built it so well
that it would take
a doomsday earthquake
to crack it down.
My father is a bricklayer.
He is a house built
with an invincible frame—
filled with bricks and mortar.
So as I drive down M street
and turn right up Wisconsin,
scuttling to another appointment
in another office,
I look in the rear view window
and adjust the earring in my ear.
I'm a different man than Father,
but I can't pass a truck of brick,
or a brick sidewalk, or a brick anything,
without thinking how much I am like him.

FLIGHT

A baby blackbird
falls from a nest.
He struggles
to fly and fails.
My father picks him up,
sticks him in a cage,
puts him in the basement.
The blackbird refuses
the worms I offer him,
the same with flax seeds.
Father mashes leftover bread,
takes the blackbird
in his bricklayer hands,
feeds him mouth to beak.
This goes on for weeks
until the blackbird
reconsiders the seed
and drinks from his bottle.

One morning
before dropping
me at school,
Father pulls the blackbird
out of his cage.
The bird bites
the ungloved
calloused fingers.
Father does not flinch.
"It's time to release him."
"What if he can't fly?"
"He will fly," Father says,
pushing open the screen door,
advancing into the backyard.

With both hands,
he throws the blackbird
into the cold, crisp air,

wills him
toward a maple branch.
The blackbird hesitates
then opens his wings.

My Father and Shakespeare at the Sylvan Amphitheater

Although my father never approved of acting,
he came to see every play I was in.
His favorites were A Midsummer Night's Dream
and Macbeth. In the dream play,
I was stuttering Snug, the joiner,
one of the rude mechanicals,
and in the Scottish play, I was loyal,
valiant Macduff, as in "lay on."

My father's choices bewildered me—
he spoke a broken English at best,
and the only thing he read
was the front page of the paper.
As for writing, he could barely print.
Perhaps it was the combination
of spectacle and verse and sunset,
each competing for attention.
I once pressed him for an answer.
"Why those two plays?"
He thought a minute, shrugged,
and said he couldn't say,
then added, "They're two good plays."

Hitler's trains

ran through Portugal
while my grandfather beat
my father until he bled.

The second of eight,
Father was better known
as *testa ferro*, iron head.
The eldest, Joaquim,
took all the favors,
but even he left for America.

It was 1942, Father was 17,
and the only way out
was the Merchant Marines.
The plan was to jump ship
in New York.

Over the Atlantic,
he played brisca
with the other sailors,
who used lice to bet with.

In the crow's nest,
gunmen waited for Nazi planes
and shot down their bombs
before they hit the deck.

On a calm still day,
bombs from a U-boat
burst beneath them.
Father jumped onto a life raft.
Hours later, he was rescued
by another merchant ship.

When he reached New York,
the city that gleamed like a statue at dawn,
Joaquim was there waiting in a car.

In the year of my father's death,
I asked him, "Did you know
what was happening to the Jews?"
"Yes," he said,
"but there was nothing we could do,
and I just wanted to be free."

WHY I SANG AT DINNER

I was not permitted a word at dinner
because you were too hot from laying
brick in the sun to bear the voices
of children and Mother too tired
to oppose you. My sister and brother,
five and six years older, had graduated
in allowance to one sentence
and on your good days two.
Sometimes I ventured a phrase,
but you pushed me down quick.
"You no speak. You have no responsibility."
The r in responsibility you would hit
with a rough Portuguese trill.
Your own father used to beat you
with a rope until you bled.
You vowed never to repeat this.
You had no need.

Still, I wanted to loosen the knot
between your brows and find
the soft place within you.
I watched how playing your accordion
for hours into the night soothed you.
Above the keys in gleaming silver
cursive was written *Excelsior.*
Since the accordion weighed too much
to pick up, I began to sing—
often in the middle of dinner.
Slenderly, I quavered out tunes
you liked from Lawrence Welk.
Sometimes I just sang *Excelsior.*
No one said anything.
How could they?
I continued without looking up.
You neither stopped me nor softened.
One evening when I was thirteen I gave up.
My new male voice was starting to break in,
and I couldn't care anymore.

FAST

Leaping like a little horse,
your barks first high and yelping,
then low, low growling and threatening,
your teeth bared and poised for piercing—
you were amorous as a hunter.
I should have kept you on a leash.
I should have taught you the difference
between cars and rabbits.
But you never were obedient.
You never would listen to me.

Was it Father or was it you? Father
who drove too fast or you who ran too fast?
Who was to blame for your catch in the wheel?
Father ran out to find you
and you were still alive, still breathing.
He turned you over and you looked at him,
as if he were God, as if you could ask,
"Why did you kill me?"

I too chase fast cars and never listen.
Unleashed and leaping like a horse,
and growling like an amorous hunter,
I will chase a bright one
only to catch in the wheel.
My father, my God will run
to find me and turn me over and
I will still be alive and breathing
and I will ask him,
"Why did you kill me?"

Hell, you were tired of waiting in the Chevy

for your money-spending wife in Toys R' Us—
damn, you had to drive her everywhere,
and in that God-awful Christmas season
with traffic clogging up every mile of road,
and in the blasted cold, cursing the gas
you were wasting, running the heater
every five minutes, not to mention,
the odd little son sitting in the back,
too sensitive for a boy, needed a lot
of toughening up, shit, your whole day
wasted, could have gone hunting,
you were going to put an end to this—
so you turned to your kid and told him,
"Robbie, you know there's no Santa Claus."

FATHER AND SON

I was young and beautiful,
and I'd just won
the Source Off-The-Wall Award
for my unorthodox rendition
of Othello. (I was white,
Desdemona was black—
there are so many variations on hate.)

I was poor, living at home,
and attempting a career.
In the kitchen, Father
read the paper and rolled
his eyes to heaven.
"You should work any job
you can get your hands on."

(In Salir do Porto,
each day was a fight
for fish and bread.
Endless labor in the sun
darkened his olive skin
until he was taken for black.)

"No, I can't," I said,
determined to hold fast
to a dream under the burning lights.
Father turned his back and said,
"I wish you would commit suicide."

TAKEN

It was mostly the color of his skin,
but he was also an immigrant
with wavy hair
and a poor laborer
with poorer English.
The sum was
he was often
taken for black.
It was the forties
and differences
were not distinguished.
His father-in-law
wouldn't attend his wedding
at Saint Aloysius
in Swampoodle, D.C.,
but stood across the street,
leaning against a lamppost,
smoking a cigarette.

Once when I was in my twenties,
I answered the phone and said hello.
"Let me talk to that goddamn nigger,"
a man said. I hung up.
I had never heard him called that.
The phone rang again. I answered.
The same voice said.
"I'd like to speak to José Christiano."
My face burned red
but I called for my father.
He got on the phone and broke
into riotous laughter. It was a joke—
a big joke between friends.
Only I wasn't in on it.

CATALYST

Home early, I'd just turned the key in the lock.
The door wasn't completely open when I saw him—
his large bricklayer frame shaken by sobs.
I took one step in. Mother was behind him.
The bulwark was crumbling. "The cancer is terminal,"
Mother said. My father came up to me and said,
"Can you forgive me? I've been a bad father."
I'd always wanted to forgive him but he had never
been sorry. "Hug your father," my mother said.
His body took in my tenuous hug. "Lung cancer,"
he said. "That's what it is. The doctors say
I have a couple of years." It turned out to be one.
Dying was the only way he could change.

BUT HAPPY

I needed to keep saying
hopeful things to him.
I said, "When you have
another remission,
you can go back to Portugal."
"No," he said. "This is my home."
He kept turning over his story—
how he was born into poverty,
the nights without dinner or supper,
no shoes until he was a teenager.
He couldn't go to school,
had to work in the fields.
The first of eight to leave,
he brought each of his sisters over,
watched each one until
they found work and a husband.
He had everything he wanted,
but in the last three days,
in that last return to childhood,
as I sat and rubbed his back,
and closed my ears
to the rattling in his chest,
he turned to me and said,
"We were poor but we were happy."

LEAVING SALIR

My father has returned
to Salir do Porto—a last wave
to a capriciously turning tide.
The villagers leave off
do Porto, and just say Salir,
meaning *to leave.*
I look over him as if
he might suddenly break.

He sees everything and everyone
as if for the first time—
the little old women in black,
the café card games of brisca,
the neighbor he once ignored,
the Uncle who hid him
from his angry father,
the fat flies at the butcher shop,
the fadistas singing of lost love.
I see little and stay in my room.

On the last morning I take to the beach.
I take to the beach and open my eyes,
I am alone with the kelp and the shells,
the sun in the air and the air in the sun,
the sand still sleeping like tarnished silver,
I am alone with the salt tinted sea—
alone with the two cliffs which part
and allow the Atlantic to begin,
the repeating, shimmering waves that care
little for the passing of fathers and sons.

Salir, you are beautiful
and I have not seen you.
Salir, you are beautiful
and I must leave you.

FATIMA

The road to Fatima is hard.
In the mountains
the road is full of bends.
I am with my mother and father,
but mostly I am with my father.
Our driver, Mario,
a guide from
my father's village,
is doing what he can
to navigate through
cars and pilgrims.
He points to the new road
they're trying to build—
the future shortcut
which doesn't appear
to be an improvement.

The sun beats and pulsates
against the pavement.
O sol bate.
The pilgrims say if you
look up long enough
you will go blind.

The entrance gate says,
Enter here as a pilgrim,
in several languages,
and further down,
No dogs allowed.

A gypsy with her two children
sits on the steps.
She cradles her baby boy
who is naked
save for a scant t-shirt.
"We have enough to eat,"
says the daughter,

counting coins.
A fifty scudo piece
drops from my hand.

In the open air church
a well-fed stray dog
stirs from his siesta.
Bells chime out
Fatima's Cove,
the hymn I have heard
since I was a boy.
On the 13th of May,
in the Cova da Iria.
Ave, Ave Maria.
A rosary is being said,
A rosary is always being said.
I light a votive on a candle pyre
where so many intentions are aflame.

The apparitions in 1917
began at the Cova da Iria—
Irene's Cove.
Seventy years later,
only the tree remains.
Various crutches support
its aging limbs.

Above the holm oak, she appeared—
a girl in blue, not yet sixteen.
The three children
minding their sheep asked,
"Who are you?"
"I am the Lady of the Rosary."
 "Are you willing to suffer?" the young lady asked.
"Suffer to save others?"
Francisco, Jacinta, and Lucia said yes.

Mario takes us
to the house of the children—

any strong wind
could tear it down,
the floorboards,
stick up and out—
no two going the same direction,
the ceiling, patched in places,
tilts unexpectedly down like a mistake.

This could be the house
Jesus said was built on sand.
This is the bed where Francisco
died of influenza.
This is the window where Jacinta
cried out to her cousin Lucia.
This is the door that sorrow cut and opened.

Outside
I struggle to focus
my camera.
A withered peasant saunters
out of the house and stands
in the doorway.
He's going to end up
in my picture.
Mario informs me
that he is the brother
of Francisco and Jacinta.
The frame is centered and I snap.
I don't ask him if he minds.
I walk across the road towards him,
even though the cab is waiting.
I extend my hand
and he takes it.
He knows I am a pilgrim.
I would like to ask him
to pray for me,
but he looks so poor,
maybe I should be praying for him.
I look at him through the cab window,

uncurling my fingers in a wave.
He looks back at me—
his face deeply weathered with lines.
The cab pulls softly away.
Mario whispers,
"This place is a mystery."

In Lucia's backyard,
at the bottom of a hill,
the angel Gabriel appeared,
and a spring issued forth from the rocks.
"Pray constantly," the angel said.
An old woman stands at the well,
offering pilgrims water from the spring.
She uses three clear glasses.
We all drink—my father,
my mother, Mario, and me.
"She is the niece of Lucia," Mario says,
as he retreats uphill to the cab.

I am alone with the woman
as poverty and silence wait on us
in the heat of the mid-afternoon.
I cannot fathom how I have managed
to meet these two relatives,
when thousands come here
every year and never do.

I ask the woman,
"Senora, por favor, você rezar por nos?"
"Senora, please, you to pray for us."
I would like to conjugate the verb rezear
but it seems a risky irregular verb.
"Sim, vou rezar," "Yes, I will pray," she replies
in what I believe is the conversational future tense.
I take courage. In decent Portuguese I say,
"We are suffering.
My father has lung cancer."
She is listening.

She understands suffering.
"Nossa Senora é útil," she says.
Our Lady is something or another.
I nod my head as if I understand.
She knows I don't
but is far too polite to indicate it.
I kiss her on both cheeks
and catch up with my father,
who is winded and still climbing.

"Father, what does 'útil' mean?"
"What?"
"What does útil mean?"
I stress the accented "u"
to make myself understood.
"My English is not too good,"
he says—then it comes to him.
"It means *helpful*."

SAINT JOSEPH AND THE BOY JESUS

after the painting by Josefa de Óbidos

The boy Jesus is guiding his foster father,
holding his hand as they walk along
a path of stone. Joseph is not old,
not white and bewildered,
his face still has a rose blush and his hair
is thick and black, but his shoulders
are weary, so weary and his face downcast.
Above the pair, the sun is descending
as gathering winds bend the pines.
Jesus, a soft, glowing boy of ten,
topped by a halo of gold spikes,
his face like an angelic girl,
his tunic a flowing pink,
leads Joseph calmly toward the viewer.
Soon they will step out of the picture.

In the last year of my father's life,
we made a pilgrimage to Fatima.
In the dry, August mountain air,
José Christiano, weary with cancer,
turned to me and asked,
"What shall I pray for?"
We paused before the holm oak tree,
faltering with age. Years before,
my pastor told me Joseph died
with Jesus by his side,
with Jesus holding his hand.
"Pray to Saint Joseph for a good death,"
I said, and held his hand,
not like the cherubic boy Jesus,
but like a beggar asking for change.

Josefa de Óbidos painted
Saint Joseph and the Boy Jesus
a few miles from the pine wood shack

where my father was born.
Josefa's father taught her
to paint the soul in every face.
My father spent a lifetime
to find the face of his soul.
After the onset of illness,
Josefa's father came to depend on her,
and here his story ends.
History will not tell us more.
Did she hold his weary hand
as they walked down the path,
the winds threatening
and the night falling?

THE MIRROR

Funerals are pretty compared to death,
Blanche Dubois says before unleashing
a litany of the dead. No one wants
to hear about death. Even my favorite cousin
snapped at me and said, "I read the email."
Perhaps the news acts as a mirror,
and the mirror says you have to do this too.
You have to leave this earth, this home,
this Belle Reve, Tara, McMansion,
ranch, condo, hovel, cardboard box.
I asked my doctor why it was taking
my father such a long time
to die of cancer. She answered,
Dying is hard on a body.

ONE SONG

"Would it be all right if he played his accordion?"
My mother, brother, sister and I closed in.
We knew he was "terminal," but what
exactly could he do between now and then?
My sister had asked the question. The oncologist,
retreating behind his glasses, said he thought
it would be safe if he played one song a day.
After all, the accordion was a weight
upon his lungs. Any more was a risk.

My father had another life in mind.
He began playing music in nursing homes.
The sick and the old didn't know about his cancer,
but their chests lightened with wheezy waltzes.
Five days before his last, barely able to stand,
he gave them a half-hour concert.

DAD AND THE SUPER BOWL

There were two choices.
Either you could play soccer
or fight a bull. That was sports in Portugal.
So it was soccer—the acrobatics
of flying through the air and punting
a ball with your head. Far better
than risking death by goring
or at the very least
getting your best clothes red.
A good choice for a kid
with a lot of muscle and no money.

And then he came to America
where soccer was exchanged
for earning, marrying, and raising.
As the older decades set in,
he took up with the Redskins.
That was in their better days.
But even back then, scoring
the big win, the Super Bowl,
was dicey. Still he, like others,
believed—fervently and devoutly.
One Super Bowl John Riggins
messed up and my father threw up.
He said it was like watching God make a mistake.

And then there was cancer.
He approached his last Super Bowl
with outrageous hope and famously said,
"If the Redskins don't win
the Super Bowl this year
I'm gonna die."
They didn't and he did.

MUINOS

Portugal is the home of windmills. No country has more. When Don Quixote fought against the windmills, he was in Portugal. That was during the years of loss when Portugal was no longer Portugal. She had lost her King. Sebastian the First disappeared like so many promises in the fray of battle. Spain swept in and took over. For decades, the Portuguese waited for Sebastian to come back. He never did.

It is against the law to destroy or deface windmills. "Muinos" they're called. Once you begin to look for muinos, they're everywhere. Muinos mark the miles. When my grandmother made bread, which was every other day, she would get up before sunrise and walk a long way to the grain mill to buy flour. Then she would come home and start the bread. She did this before the children had risen.

When cancer was completing my father's days, my brother and I bought him an ornamental windmill for the garden. My brother hammered it into the hard winter ground in the midst of a prickly nest of junipers. My father could see the windmill from his window as he lay in bed.

Even a slight wind would cause the rainbow wheel to turn, and a moderate wind would push the red tail in a new direction. Father was depleted but the windmill held his gaze. Three days later, he died in the middle of the night. That morning I raised the blinds and looked at the windmill. The rainbow was turning, turning without ceasing.

SALIR DO PORTO

Little port of Portugal
leaving port of Portugal,
leaving port of my father's hometown—
what words shall I find to describe
the dull gray of your sand
or the uneasy clouds which seem
to inch so close to the ground?
What words to describe
the seaweed tides of your bay,
the blue green that washes
down the deep of me?
What words to describe the great parting
between two rocky cliffs
that breaks and breathes in the Atlantic
or the music in your line
of cabanas striped rose and lime?
What words for the salt breeze
that wipes across the wetness
on the back of my neck
during the siestas of the midday sun?
What words for the joyous uplooking
of the olive skinned families
who bedeck your banks?
What words could convey
how you bring back
my father in your waves?

I will not find the words to say
when I stand at the point
where my father as a young man
used to jump into your bay.
I will not find the words to say
how he swam unfettered by clothes,
determined as a Portuguese man-of-war,
often against the tide, strong
and resilient against the current
where the bay unites with the Atlantic,

and the Atlantic unites with the world.
I will not find the words to recapture
how he reached the shores of America
glittering with the possibility of work,
and how he worked and worked and worked.
I will not find the words to say how he loved
and failed to love those who loved him.
I will not be able to say how on his deathbed,
I felt him dip into the Atlantic Styx
and reel away in his olive skin back to you.
I will not find the words to say to you—
little leaving port of Portugal
to whom I am forever returning.
What words could ever say
how he left me who cannot swim,
standing on your shore of sorrow?

Memorial Day

In the morning sun, I find Father's lot
    and fresh is the grief which pricks me.
Bending down, I pull out the weeds
    and dust off his name.
So soon for dust and weeds
    to encroach on so recent a man.
As I straighten out his plot,
    a picture from the family album
    poses before me.
Father is tossing his baby son in the air.
His muscular arms, hands,
    chest stretch upwards.
I am laughing—my mouth open to a smile,
    my body suspended.
In the next frame he will catch me.

And so I do my best
    to keep neat his grave.
The cemetery will not let me
    plant flowers here.
I do not mind much
    even though I am a gardener.
I give him bright plastic flowers
    of red and gold.
I know they will not fade.

RELATIVES

AVÓ

I thought she was immortal.
She was over a hundred, after all.
Falas devogar. Speak slowly,
I would say and she'd oblige.
I'd sit next to her on the couch—
the one covered in plastic,
where she'd be watching a TV show
she could no longer see
in a language she never learned.
If she were still in her nineties
she'd be in the kitchen making
o roz dolce, the sweet rice pudding—
spreading it with a butter knife
into a even layer on a dinner plate,
then squinting to etch a windmill in cinnamon.
She'd recite jingles all the while, inventing rhymes
to go with the names of her children,
Roberto—Doberto, Ida—Jerida, Zé—Bé.

She knew every word of her boyfriend's last letter.
They were both star-crossed sixteen. She'd close
her eyes and intone the words of his rejection.
 "My suffering," he said, "is equal to that of Christ on the cross."
Beginning in her forties, she wore the eternal black dress
of a widow even though she was only divorced.
Sometimes she'd let my hamster crawl across her black shawl.
On the dining room table, a doily of crocheted swans
floated across the nights without food.
She was always reading catalogs
but never called them catalogs.
She'd say, "I am reading a book."
In times of plenty, there would be one scoop
of vanilla ice cream in a coffee mug.

At a hundred and one, she still refused to give up
her apartment even though she was no longer
well enough to live there. As long as it was there,

she lived. Just a decade earlier,
she sat beside the bed of her son
as he underwent the chemo that would fail.
She cried for weeks, visited his grave, and then went on.
She always went on. She was immortal.

Grandfather's Mistress

When I arrived, age thirteen, first time
out of America, she met me in the dark
at the train station in Salir. I kept looking
and looking for her among the host
of unfamiliar faces. Then I remembered
she was a dwarf and looked down.
She was shouting my name. I wasn't
supposed to like her. After all, she
wasn't Grandmother. Avó was a saint,
the matriarch against all odds—she had
suffered both Grandfather and poverty.
But when I was ill, Merrita butchered
her hen and made me chicken soup.
She made my bed every day to spoil me.
She smiled when she spoke to me.

EATING CHICKEN IN PORTUGAL

My sister, JoAnna Maria,
is petting the chickens
in someone's front yard.
This is her first visit to Salir.
Half of the village is related to her,
and she barely speaks Portuguese.
She strokes a golden chicken like a pet,
and talks to it in that voice
reserved for animals.

A hearty woman
barrels out of the house.
She's got to be a cousin.
Everyone is a cousin. Prima Maria,
Prima Teresa, Prima Luisa.
She goes up to JoAnna Maria
and says, *tu quieres*, you like,
using the intimate tu
and pointing to the fowl.
My sister says *sim*.
Then Prima grabs
the chicken by the throat,
slaps it down on a table,
pulls out a convenient axe,
and whop. Without wasting breath,
she plucks out the feathers
while the legs are still kicking.
This is her way of asking my sister to lunch.
And my sister, blinking at the butchery,
her nose recoiling at the guts,
knows she must, must stay.
Prima will not have chicken tomorrow
or the next day or even the next.
Tomorrow will be kale soup
and the next day beans,
perhaps, a few sardines
if she puts her coins together.

Chicken is her special Sunday supper,
her husband's return from the sea,
her daughter's engagement,
her son's baptism.

And so my sister, JoAnna Maria,
sits down at the table,
and turns her head away
from the blood stains out the window,
and slowly cuts into the breast with a knife.

RUNNING MACKEREL

Carapau Corrindo! Carapau Corrindo!
Running Mackerel! Running Mackerel!

I still hear the calls
of the fisherwomen of Nazaré
as they ran into our village
dressed in their seven skirts,
balancing baskets of mackerel
squiggling with life
atop their heads.

I asked my mother,
"Why do they cry out,
running mackerel, running mackerel?"
and she answered,
"That's because, Brancinha,
the women run to get here."
I never believed her.

Half a lifetime
and a grown son later,
I visited Nazaré,
and stopped at the café.
"Can you tell me," I asked the waitress,
"why your fisherwomen
used to call out,
running mackerel, running mackerel?"
The young lady looked blank,
the history lost from her time.
"There's an old women in the back.
Perhaps she would know."

I approached the greatly lined
woman in black.
"Senhora, can you tell me something?
I'm Branca Christiano from Salir do Porto,
nearly five kilometers from here.

When I was little your fisherwomen
would come barefoot singing out,
running mackerel, running mackerel.
Why did they say running?"
The old woman smiled and spoke
in a voice coated with calluses,
"Yes, they did run, and I know
because I was one of those women.
We would wait on the shore
for the men in the boats to arrive.
We were so poor we couldn't waste a minute.
We tied our scarves into a frame for our heads,
pushed the basket on top, and ran all the way
without a stop to Salir do Porto.
Those fish were barely out of the ocean."

COKE MEMORIES

As I savor the sip of this Coke,
I can feel the decay progressing
inside my mouth. I would like
to give it up, but I can't.

Disabled by a breakdown,
an actor I know
survived off the residuals
of his Coke commercial,
the tag line of which was
"I don't want anything
if I can't have the real thing."

My Great Aunt Anna
remembers when the real thing
first came out. She says,
"Back then, it made you feel
really good. It had zip to it.
I think it was those small glass bottles."

In 1886, Coke first appeared
as a patented medicine—
a digestive and headache remedy
as well as an impotence aid.
Each glass contained nine
milligrams of cocaine.

Once, my friend Poala,
stuck in a mental ward,
had a stomach ache,
and didn't want to speak
to a doctor anymore.
I brought her a coke.

My father in his little
Portuguese village
of Salir do Porto,

heard of Coke
when he was a teenager
struck with acne
spreading across his face.

He pedaled barefoot
on a bicycle
through miles and miles
of poverty and sorrow
to buy a Coke
because he believed
it would cure him.

UNCLE ROBBIE IS HERE

He flew in from Hartford
for my niece's wedding.
He asks if I wouldn't mind taking him
to see the cherry trees around the tidal basin
because he oh so loves them,
and could we see the bonsai exhibit at the arboretum,
and does that Portuguese restaurant Tavira still exist on Connecticut,
way down past Chevy Chase, yes, he knows it's out of the way,
but they make the best eel stew, and it's so hard to get eel stew these days,
and they make tripe, back home they make tripe all the time, which reminds him
to ask you to stop by the Spanish market on the way to the wedding
because they have good cured cod there, and would I mind on Saturday
taking him to some tag sales, he collects short wave radios and once bought
a good one from someone's lawn in Northern Virginia and has never forgotten it.
As for Sunday, he would like to take a drive in Alexandria because he once found
a street there that was covered in hydrangeas called Inês Street, and while he's not
completely sure that the street actually exists, or maybe it does, but in another city
like Providence or Lisbon, he would like to check it out just the same,
so he can be sure. And by the way, what am I doing after work on Monday?
He would like to go see the Lee-Custis house again because he says
history is everything, and while we are there, we should pay a visit
to Kennedy's grave because there was a President for you.
I say, "I'm not sure I can fit all that in." He asks why.
"Uncle Robbie, do you remember King Sebastian, the First of Portugal?
Do you remember how he went all the way to Morocco to conquer the Moors?"
"Yes," he says. "Remember how he tried to convert the Muslims and failed?"
"Yes." he says. "Then you know where I am going with this."
Next summer he's coming for a month.

Uncle Robbie And
The Portuguese National Football Team

Do you watch Portuguese soccer?
No, I don't watch sports.
So, you don't know about
Cristiano Rinaldo, Luis Figa,
or Rui Costa?
No, I don't.
So, you don't know about
Nani, Deco, or Simão?
No, I don't know about them.
I guess this means you don't
watch The World Cup,
and I guess you don't know
about the Grupo de Morte,
the Group of Death,
or how Carlos Queiroz
led Portugal to the second round.
No, I've never watched
The World Cup.
Then you don't know
that I called
the Portuguese Embassy
to discuss the match.
They said the staff
came in at 5 A.M.
so they could watch
the game against Korea
in real time.
Portugal won—7 to 0.
Oh, I said. Congratulations.

UNCLE ROBBIE AND EVA PERON

"Eva Peron died a few years ago,"
Uncle Robbie said, unexpectedly.
We were on the sofa,
drinking anisette at the time.
It was a spring day, early
in the twenty-first century.
"If by a few years ago
you mean the fifties
then you're right," I said.
"No," he said. "It was recently."
Now I owned a record
of Weber's musical
which opens with the day
of her death. I put it on.
Uncle Robbie listened
as Che Guevara announced
the date as July 26, 1952,
and the chorus moaned
Santa Evita in dirge time.
"That's just a story that someone made up.
I can't believe that. It's on a record."
At this point my brother John,
sitting silently in the easy chair,
reading the Post, got up and went down
to the basement to retrieve the letter "P"
from the Encyclopedia Britannica.
When he returned he sat between
Uncle Robbie and me and said,
"I have the truth but I'm not sure
it's going to make any difference."

UNCLE ROBBIE AT THE THANKSGIVING TABLE

It has taken a great deal of effort
to get my aunts and uncles
and cousins in one place,
and now, at the dinner table,
it has taken even more effort
to get them to be quiet for grace.
I hold my aging aunt's wrinkled hand
and my great niece's unwrinkled one.
I quickly get in the prayer
before another interruption.
And then there's this silence—
an acknowledgement that we
are indeed family, that we
are actually related, and perhaps
there is even the pretence that we are one,
and if not one, at least united.

Then Uncle Robbie speaks.
"You know, yesterday, I reached
into the pocket of my jacket,
my blue one, not my grey one,
you know my blue one that I got
in the Lisbon airport in '95,
and I found my schedule
for physical therapy. I had already
missed an appointment. I called
the office and asked them
if I had to pay for the appointment,
and they said I did, and a late charge
as well. Well, I said, how much
is the late charge, that's what I want
to know. How much do you think
it was?"

There is no answer.
The buzz of talk has resumed
as the clatter of plates

and silverware fill the room.
Uncle Robbie drops physical therapy
and begins to expound
on the demerits of the expensive
new bus station in East Hartford,
"A complete waste. That money
should've gone to the homeless shelter.
But does anyone care,
does any care, I ask you?"
He says this with such force
that he blows out the candle
in front of him. I strike a match
and relight it and move the candle
away from him. He continues.

ABOUT SOME FIRES

It is the middle of August. I am riding through the bumpy Portuguese countryside with my cousin Fernanda. By nightfall we'll be back in my father's village. A smoky dust mists the road as I turn in my seat.

A large patch of brush is flaming by the side of the road. Fernanda rolls up the windows of the VW so the smoke can't seep in. I am thinking, *My god, the farmers. Won't their crops catch?*

A little further on another blaze is spreading through the fields. I hear the sizzle through the closed windows. Fernanda straightens her hair in the rear view mirror.

"Fernanda, excuse me, but we seem to be driving through a fire."

She touches the medallion of Mary round her neck and accelerates slightly. "It hasn't rained here in months. Sometimes it just happens with the heat and all."

"What about the farmers?"

"Sometimes they light the fires. They rent the land and the land doesn't produce. If the farm catches fire they don't have to pay the rent."

"But aren't fires dangerous?"

"These usually burn out by themselves."

We drive on as the smoke evaporates into the thin taut air. By evening we are in Salir. Before bed I walk out to the dock. Across the dark glistening bay are the crooked hills of São Martinho. Fires periodically spear up on the hilltops. The flames sparkle like candles on a baby's cake. I watch them a long while, then leisurely walk back into my father's home to sleep without fear.

THE DRAGONS OF CALIFORNIA

It was one of those impossibly hot, dry, California summers. Wildfire sparked everywhere. We had seen this before. In my father's village, we spent nights watching brush fires across the bay ignite, evolve, and die out. They were routine, commonplace, small, confined. But in California, they were positively Old Testament. Fires burned for a month. Smoke rose for weeks more. They said you could drive for miles through burnt out forests and hear absolutely nothing. And we, my brother and I, both grown men, sat and watched it all from the east coast in the comfort of our TV room. Finally, Johnny confided, "You know what is causing those fires, don't you?" "No." "It's these flying creatures." My face must have revealed my disbelief. "Let's go to Borders and I'll show you pictures of them." Borders was just blocks from where we lived. Johnny rummaged through their photography books. Frustrated, he gave up. He started rifling through the illustrated fantasy books where he found what he was looking for and what he was looking for was a dragon. The dragon was not as big as a helium balloon or tall as a house or round as a Frisbee. He was the size of a standard horse, albeit a flying horse. He was your classic dragon, the dragon you expect, the dragon of your childhood. Green and scaled, he was flying and his mouth was open and he was breathing out flames. "There, that's what causing the fires." Not the heat, not the drought, not a misguided kid on a dune buggy, not a camper and a campfire. It was a dragon, prehistoric and yet still alive after all this time. Alive and real at last. And he was real, real to Johnny. Many years earlier a professional told me my brother was ill. He was delusional. But that was an explanation and what can an explanation explain? I only know that now my brother has died the dragons of California are gone too. God only knows how I grieve their going.

Everything

Those African violets I grew tired of watering,
My first, second, and third hamster,
My favorite golden finch,
The goldfish my cat never captured,
Two of the Beatles,
The summer of endless zucchini,
The silver carp we caught for dinner,
Frost's birches and Chopin's nocturnes,
My memory of The Remembrance of Things Past,
My first boyfriend,
Le Bon Cafe where we met every day,
My capacity for love,
Winter's last reprise,
Even you, my brother—
as you sit down in Culpepper Library,
open your laptop and sip your coffee,
totally unaware of the stroke that will take you.

HERITAGE

In the dark blue of the Azores
you seek the simple staple called linguiça—
a sausage much like chorizo.
The street vendor looks at you
as if you were Sancho Panza
explaining Aristotle,
which brings to mind
the time you saw an Aztec princess
order a pizza in the Bronx.
When Domino's arrived late,
she told the pizza guy,
"I am an Aztec Princess."
He said, "Don't put on airs."
It's hard to come from an ancient lineage.
One would think, oh how great to list
the forefathers right down to Adam,
but by the time you do your laptop
falls off the desk, and with frank futility
you realize it is easier to settle for vanilla pie.
And even then, when you are enjoying your first slice,
the ghosts drop in for an after dinner drink. It turns out
they haven't stopped by to look at your stamps
or check their names for accuracy in the Bible. It's loss.
They want you to strip them of their loss. So you ask
your best friend over, who is a medium, and you coax them
with coals and sage. You speak to them in their native tongue.
You tell them you can't do what they've asked. You never could.
You tell them what you've always wanted to tell them.
You tell them to go home. And they do not answer. They are your family.
The best they can do is to limp away into the vast dark blue forest of incredibility.

PORTUGAL AND THE WORLD

Brother Portugal

His face stares out to me
    across the Atlantic,
    beyond plains of time
    and windmills of war,
    above fields of despair
    and through threshing room doors.
His face stares out to me,
    not wrecked by devastation,
    or destroyed by fire,
    not fraught with famine
    or soured with sickness,
    not crushed, not blemished,
    not bruised.
His face stares out to me,
    not organized, not nuclearized,
    not Americanized, not Communized,
    sim democratismo ou facismo,
    without politics or sorrow,
    not broken, but whole,
    free spirited and free souled
    despite the universe.
His face stares out to me,
    through the discovered
    and the undiscovered,
    and who I see is not alien,
    and who he is, is not foreign.
    He is my own reflection.
    He is my brother, myself.

LEAP

Some say it was the devil, others say it was a deer,
but it appeared as a deer leaping in the thick fog
of morning. Dom Fuas, the king's brother,
had gathered his bow and arrow and mounted
his gray mare. His cloak of burnished gold
rippled in the sea breeze. The deer was the most
exquisite he'd ever seen. She turned back to look
at him with the most human eyes and jumped
high into the mist. The prince followed. Sensing
danger, she blindly leapt over a precipice—
the towering cliff of Nazaré. The mare also leapt.
In a flash of reckoning the prince discerned his peril.
He prayed to Mary of Nazareth and the mare froze
in midair. Her hind legs had not left the ledge
and she reared back to safe ground. You can still
see the imprint of a hoof before the descent.
It doesn't look like much, but then again,
it's nine centuries old.

THE CARTOGRAPHY OF PORTUGAL

In this map we call the universe, Portugal will place itself at the center.
Her kings and queens will purple the parchment and seep into Africa,
Asia, America. Pessoa will never write a poem as powerful, Camões
will never create a grander mythology, and Amália, garbed in black,
will never sing a sadder fado. The river Douro and the river Tagus
contain the hand of Moses and the hand produces plague and pestilence.
The rivers run vermilion against the lemon skies of the breaking centuries.
St. Anthony, do not leave us. We need our martyrs here, not in Morocco
or Padua. Captain Da Gama, what do the spices of India have to offer?
Why turn the Cape? There will be crusades and we will lose our king,
lose our kingdom, and Spain, ever anxious, will take us when
we are not looking. We will glove our hand and put on the mask,
turn our back, and bind the natives. Our Jews will hide their names
in baptism, set sail for a new exile, or hang in a flame of faith.
Angola, Goa, and Mozambique will flower like a dream in an opium den
without a thought to the day of awakening. Democracy brazen
as a carnation in April will blaze through the woods of fascism.
For a long time now, we have tried to balance democracy and fascism
and we are tired. Plant the lemon trees along the coast of the Algarve.
In the springtime they will spread their fragrance.

THE DIVISION OF THE WORLD

You, Portugal,
can have all the lands south
of the Canary Islands.
You, Spain,
can have all the lands west and south
of the Azores and Cape Verde.
All the lands in India
that currently or at one time
belonged to Spain, go to Spain,
To Portugal all the islands of the Maluku.
Portugal, you can also take Brazil.
Spain, America is yours.
Portugal, Asia now belongs to you—
that entire hemisphere is yours.
All unknown and undiscovered lands
can be claimed by whoever gets there first.
So say the Papal Bulls.
So says the Treaty of Tordesillas.
So says Sixtus the Fourth.
So say the Crowns of Aragon and Castile.
So says John the Second of Lisbon.
But King Francis the First of France,
sitting on his throne,
chewing a wad of tobacco
and surveying the maps,
spits and says,
"Show me Adam's will!"

THE WARS OF ROSEMARY AND MARJORAM

My father's town was founded by two families—the Cristãos and the Alecrims.
The two families intermarried. My grandparents were first cousins.
We all turned out inbred, depressed, and nearsighted.

In 1497, Manoel the First of Portugal demanded that all Jews convert or leave.
Some left. Some converted. Some pretended. Some changed their names
to the names of herbs. They were called the New Christians or Conversos—
the converted ones.

Somewhere along the line in America, Cristão proved too challenging
and turned into Christiano. I came to hate it. I always thought Christiano
sounded like a stage name. And then there was history—
the history of Christianity to salt the wound.

In the rollicking 1730's, the toast of the Lisbon theatre
was Antonio José da Silva. He wrote delicious skits with songs
satirizing politics and the bourgeoisie. Most of his plays were for puppets.
His big hit was The Wars of Rosemary and Marjoram.
The King just adored him. His nickname was The Jew.

Every Thanksgiving my favorite cousin, Elizabet Alecrim, tells me all the dirt,
tells me how Primo Eduardo, the most handsome cousin, had a nervous
breakdown when he was eighteen because he thought his penis was too small
and that Tia Rosa's husband beats her regularly.

On October 5, 1737, Antonio and family faced an auto-da-fé.
Their black slave brought forth evidence of Judaizing. The Silvas engaged
in unorthodox fasting and Antonio secretly acquired a circumcision.
The King intervened but the Inquisition found the comedian too threatening.
He was strangled then burnt in front of his family.
That night one of his popular operettas was performed.

I invite Cousin Elizabet to sit in the seat of honor. I begin to carve
the clove studded ham. She pours herself some wine and says,
"Have I told you yet that we have Jewish blood in the family?
After all these years, I did the Ancestry thing, and well, now I know
why Alecrim means rosemary."

BARUCH OR BENEDICT

In his *Theologico-Political Treatise,*
Baruch Spinoza stated the following:
the Jews were not God's chosen people,
prophets and prophecies were dubious,
biblical interpretation usually incorrect,
the Torah flawed, the Talmud suspect,
miracles absurd, rituals meaningless,
and Christianity questionable.

His grandfather fled the Inquisition.
Manoel the First said convert, leave, or burn.
The family moved to Nantes, France
where they were also expelled.
Then they moved to Rotterdam,
and then again to Amsterdam
where they could openly practice.
At six Baruch was memorizing the Talmud.

In 1656, the Jewish community issued Baruch
the writ of cherem—the writ of excommunication.
As the words of the rite were read,
the candles in the synagogue were gradually
snuffed out so the congregation could experience
the blackness of Baruch's soul.

Let him be accursed by day and accursed by night;
accursed in his lying down and his rising up,
in his going out and in his coming in.
May the wrath and displeasure of the Lord
load him with all the curses written
in the book of the law, and raze out
his name from under the sky.

Baruch later changed his name to Benedict.
He devoted himself to the business of a lens grinder
and the elusive quest of philosophy.

He died of a lung illness brought on by breathing
the toxic dust from grinding eyeglasses.
The cherem was never revoked.

The year was 1968. I was thirteen.

"Your government isn't very good,"
Raul said. He was a 16-year-old
student who befriended me on a tour
of the south of Portugal—one silvery
beach after another, the coast jagged
with the beauty and power of stone.
We drank coffee in every café.

"Your government isn't very good.
You get one man in office and you're
stuck for four, maybe eight, years."

I didn't know what to say. I had neither
the knowledge nor experience to speak.
Still I found his words impolite.

"This Nixon you've just elected.
How can you elect such a man?"

Outside the window, waves ran over rocks.

"How about your government?" I asked.
"What is your weakness?"

Raul tensed—lines twisted
next to blemishes, his eyes
lowered to the table.

Silence filled in the space.
A separation grew.

That night I discussed the scene with Mother.

"You can't discuss the politics here.
Salazar won't permit it."

"Who?"

"The prime minister. Raul can't even criticize his government. They might throw him in prison or worse.
He's a smart boy. It's harder for him."

BLUES OF LONGING

Here, in D.C.,
I live,
I breathe,
I work in a library,
but I dream of Portugal,
    of the women blues singers,
      singing at night in their black clothes,
    of matadors who do not kill,
    of men who are fishing,
    of women who are waiting.
I dream of two roses set in a vase—
    a table laid with bread and wine.
I dream of a little boy with a dirty face
    eating a chocolate ice cream.
I dream of sand and water—silver and blue.
I dream of houses—pink and green.
I dream of things I will never see.
I close my eyes and hope to live in that sun.

MEMOIR

after the fados of Amália

I did not ask to be a fadista.
I hid myself behind cups
of wine and smoke,
knowing well
the wages of poverty,
the taste of secrecy,
the winks and whistles
at my back. Salazar declared
that every fado singer must
carry an identity card.
He called me a little creature.
But you lifted me
on an altar of incense.
You tuned your guitars
to the key of the black shawl
that covered my shoulders.
What I sang was sadness.
It was not my sadness.
It was ours.

ON HEARING THE FADO
O GENTE DA MINHA TERRA
OH PEOPLE OF MY LAND

Yes, this sorrow is mine.
Yes, this sorrow is yours.
This is our beautiful destiny
and there we must go.
The guitar speaks the truth
and we know the name of the song.
We fished the ocean
and our catch was tears.
We lost a dream
and the dream was the world.
This is what we cannot deny.
Our sighs are our only tenderness.
If I could write a poem
that was merely happy
I would not be Portuguese—
I would not be one of you.
Oh my people,
let me go to church
and light my candle.
The flame is sorrow.
Oh my people,
let me sing my song
and we will call it fado.

DESTINO

We Portuguese are good at death.
You can't discover half the earth
without losing some lives.
We have carried our bodies
from the church to the graveyard.
We have gripped each other's arm and
said *Tem Coragem*. Have courage.
The blessed virgin saw
her son die on a cross.
We have skipped the embalming
and gone straight to the viewing.
In the village we don't have
money for embalming.
(Who has money for embalming?)
We only know how to attend funerals—
even the neighbors we barely know
or the cousins we no longer remember.
We only know we are all somehow related.
We have learned to stand over a pine box
and whisper, "She seems peaceful."
or "How good he looks."

We Portuguese are good at dying.
We wear black. We have always
worn black. We have worn black
for as long as black has been black.
You can't lose a continent
without learning how to dress.
We have seen the New World
and we have lost it.
We wanted Africa, Angola, Mozambique.
What did we know?
We know crying and rosaries.
We know the short march from the church bell
to the yard of alabaster.

We know the salt water that takes our lives—
how the shores of Belem, Nazaré, and Foz
are bedecked with black widows.
We Portuguese have learned to stay
in our churches. It's easier that way.
If you stay long enough you might escape.

THE MARTYRS

I

Martyrs in Nagasaki, dated 1622, color on paper, by the school
of Giovanni Niccolò, depicts the public execution of 23 Christians
in Japan. The Daimyo Hideyoshi had forbidden the Christianity
promulgated by the Spanish Jesuits and Portuguese Franciscans.
In Niccolò's version, a group of 20 monks in flowing robes stand
on a thin strip of earth. A moat has been dug around them and filled
with raging fire. Nearby, on solid ground, samurai with raised swords
are beheading missionaries. A long wood railing topped with spikes
awaits a complete collection of heads. There are already five.
Blood pours out of the headless bodies of five holy brothers.
Outside the execution area, a band of samurai keep
the crowd in order. There are hundreds watching—
a brocade of bright kimonos. Some are Japanese converts praying.
Some are foreigners—barbarians the Japanese called them.

II

In *Martyrs in Nagasaki,* the Japanese have returned
to their traditional methods of execution—burning and beheading.
Earlier they used crucifixion—a method acquired from the Christians.

February 5, 1597, marked the day of the first mass crucifixion.
If left unchecked the barbarians would take over.
26 Christians were chosen—Portuguese, Spanish, and Japanese.
They were forced to march for 30 days and their left ears were cut off.
The path to the hill of crosses facing the bay of Nagasaki was washed in blood.
Each of the 26 knew which cross was his because they were custom sized.
Each cross contained the latest Japanese innovation—rings to hold the bodies
in place.

At a predetermined time that is all time and without time,
the crosses rise in unison and drop into the waiting holes.
The crowd, numbering 4,000, prays, screams, and cries.
The youngest martyr, Louis Ibaraka, age 12,
yells out, "paradise, paradise," and "Jesus, Mary."
Martin of the Ascension prays, "Blessed be the Lord God of Israel
for he has visited and redeemed his people."

Anthony of Nagasaki sees his father and mother in the front row.
Before sunset, the samurai come to each cross to pierce each chest
with two lances. The crowd in ecstatic frenzy breaks through the guard
and rushes to the crosses with rags to mop up the new relics of holy blood.

III
By 1629, every missionary had left. Thousands of Christians had been executed.
The Daimyo believed Christianity was eradicated,
but in 1865, a French priest, arriving in Nagasaki, discovered the presence
of an underground Christian community.

ALCÁCER-QUIBIR, 1578

Sebastian the First of Portugal was nicknamed *The Desired One*.
What Sebastian desired was Morocco. He wanted Christianity
to be king or maybe he was just tired of jousting at home.
Even though he was frail and unfit for the army or even armor he hauled
over twenty thousand men to Africa. Angola, Mozambique, Malacca
were already his and they were lovely, but he was on a crusade.
The Muslims had other ideas. The king of desire stormed Alcácer-Quibir.
When it was over, the African adventure cost him eight thousand lives.
Another fifteen thousand were sold into slavery.
As for King Sebastian, he disappeared.
He was last seen battling wildly. For centuries,
the Portuguese waited for him to return.
They waited for him to return when the Spanish took over.
They waited for him to return when the earthquake flattened Lisbon,
and when the Brazilians turned godless. They waited as they lost the world.

In their grief, the Portuguese discovered an old word
and made it new again. It is both untranslatable and
the most descriptive of their character. The word is saudade.
My travel guide defines it as "a sort of ethereal, aching melancholy
that seems to yearn for something lost or unattainable."[1]
Even now they are still waiting, waiting for Sebastian.

---

[1] Baedeker's Portugal, 1983

QUAKE, 1755

It is All Saints Day
and we are at mass—
gathered like bees in a hive.
We must pray for all saints,
and not forget to pray for ourselves.
Our priests are vested in purple.
The Preparation of the Eucharist has begun.
The Lamb is prepared for the slaughter.
And then a strange frightful rumble.
The church shakes.
Our saints fall from their pedestals.
A crucifix falls and kills the priest.
Those who are lucky, the latecomers
standing in the back, escape in time.
The rumble turns to a thunderous boom
followed by the sound of an entire city collapsing—
the Manueline palace replete with gothic towers,
the Tagus Opera House with its gilded balconies,
the marble museum with its rooms
of Titians and Caravaggios,
the Corpus Christi convent we paid our tithes to.

We swarm to the Tagus River—
the river has always been our salvation—
it has padded our purse,
fed our table, salted our shakers.
And we are all here:
the society lady without her shoes,
the prostitute startled awake,
the monk without his flail,
the count with his casket of ruby,
the servant in his crimson livery,
the beggar without his crutch,
the Inquisitor without his court,
the mother with her screaming children.
In the Tagus boats and ships
are turning and rocking and weaving—

the smaller ones splinter apart.
The water is rising into a wall and
the wall is as high as the church steeple.
Those who can, run back into the collapsing city.
Many amass on the marble quay,
but then the wave crashes through
and devours everyone on it.
Christ falls from the cross.
We latch onto whatever rises—
the palace door, the gaming table,
the fractured sides of a chest,
the bow of a boat,
the torn topsail,
the jade comb,
the severed and tangled nets—
the floating remnants of our days.
And then with the force of thunder
the wave rips back into its bed,
bringing with it the living, the drowning,
the dead and the dying.

Those of us on earth
hurry past the crushed and lame,
We can only try to save ourselves.
We run into the hills of the Alfama.
The rich on horses gallop away—
foam chasing against frantic hooves.
But just when we have stopped to catch our breath,
we remember the candles lit in our churches,
the fires in our hearth, the fabric in our looms.
The fires catch quickly and the city
burns so brightly we are blinded by it.

Is this our hell, oh God?
Is this why you have brought us into the world—
to burn our city, to let us perish in flames?

Days after the last tremor shakes
and the final flames are snuffed,

and the smoke thins into nothing,
gossips in the safety of glowing Paris
will murmur of how our girls became prostitutes
and our homeless turned to looters.
By the end of All Saints Day
the soul of the city had left.
Every home was hollowed.
Every business a scatteration.
Every chapel, church, and cathedral fell.
Lisbon was our beehive
and the beekeeper had taken out all the combs,
broken them and burnt them.

MAGELLAN RENDERS JUSTICE

He was sailing the Victoria, trying to circle
the world. The King of Portugal declined
approval so he convinced the King of Spain.
His Gallic crew resented their turncoat captain.

In this very voyage of impossibility,
the ship's master, Antonio de Solomon,
was caught sodomizing the cabin boy.
The act was so common at sea

that most captains chose to ignore it.
But with a crew ready to mutiny at first cause,
Magellan resorted to Spanish law,
which found *sodomia* punishable by death.

Antonio de Solomon was tried and a date
for his execution set. In the interim
the Victoria docked in tropical Rio,
where all the native girls stripped and

swam out to meet them. Every night was ecstasy,
even though the King of Spain expressly
forbade pagan relations. A girl could easily
be bought in exchange for a shiny piece of metal.

Shortly before Christmas, in a public ceremony,
the executioner, made anonymous by a hood,
strangled Antonio de Solomon. As for the cabin boy,
two variant endings survive.

In the first, he is so severely mocked by the crew
that he jumps headlong into the ocean. In the second,
the crew throws him in.

THE PAST IS NEVER DEAD[i]

March returns like memory
and memory aches to be framed
in a melting rivulet of beauty.
But memorials are for the dead
and the dead leave nothing unsaid.
They talk through whispers,
through shrouds and shrugs,
through minds and messages,
through words, words, words.

The snow on the asphalt has melted.
What's left is black with grime and dirt and stone.
The revenants return with the pelting rain.
The revenants return again and again.

Let us take out our teacups and sit in the Florida room.
I'll pour the tea, my friend, and dispel the Virginia gloom.
Let us switch and talk of Trump and Salazar.
Let us tie our ties and swing on a swing.
The Potomac River is alive with budding cherry trees.

Psychic Bob, the medium on YouTube,
draws the curtains closed with a hush,
shuts his eyes, communes with the nether world,
flutters his lids, instinctively grabs the bag
of runes and throws them over a black cloth.
"The way is blocked. The road is covered.
Derecho, tornado, or winter storm.
There is no way out except through the cemetery."

"Father, what happened to the Jews?"
On Nine-eleven the sky was blue.

And then there are the other martyrs:
the young gay man strung up like Christ,
the Portuguese shoeshine boy drowned,
the Capital guards hunted and downed,

the cigarette seller shot, the Mexican bound,
that woman from the mosque defaced.
Hush! Good Friday happens every week.

"Father, what happened to the Jews?"

And my father, red brown in his Portuguese skin,
tired from laying brick in the sun,
rubs his worn out hands and says,
"Portugal was under Salazar
and there was nothing we could do,
and all I wanted was to find America.
It's what we all wanted—to be free."

March is the mysterious month.
Mostly dead and fully alive.
Each day unpredictable as ice.
The past isn't even past.

ⁱ Title and last line are Faulkner's.

Roberto Christiano started out his artistic life as a child actor and ended up as a writer. Along the way other arts became involved: painting, photography, and music. So far he's been a church pianist, herbalist, editor, coach, gardener, and library technician. He hopes to host many other identities before the run is over. He has been writing poems for 55 years. Sometime in the 90s, he decided to take it seriously and studied for several decades at The Writer's Center of Bethesda followed by a few years more at Politics and Prose, the notable D.C. bookstore and literary hub. Among his many teachers were Pulitzer Prize winner Henry Taylor, formalist Annie Finch, and Anne Becker, Poet Laureate Emerita of Takoma Park, Maryland. Christiano enjoys writing in a variety of genres: fiction, poetry, and drama. His poetry and fiction are continually published in literary journals, and his short plays have been produced at the Source Theatre in Washington, D.C. He was nominated by *Prairie Schooner* for the 2010 Pushcart Prize for his poem, "Why I Sang at Dinner." Christiano is also a student of haiku and tanka and was a two time finalist in *The Washington Post*'s annual springtime haiku contest. He lives in Springfield, Virginia, close enough to D.C. to be entertained but far enough away to remain sane. To keep up to date with Christiano please visit his website: www.robertochristiano.weebly.com.

www.ingramcontent.com/pod-product-compliance
Lightning Source LLC
Chambersburg PA
CBHW021156090426
42740CB00008B/1114